German Shepherds

Leo Statts

abdopublishing.com

Published by Abdo Zoom™, PO Box 398166, Minneapolis, Minnesota 55439. Copyright © 2017 by Abdo Consulting Group, Inc. International copyrights reserved in all countries. No part of this book may be reproduced in any form without written permission from the publisher. Abdo Zoom™ is a trademark and logo of Abdo Consulting Group, Inc.

Printed in the United States of America, North Mankato, Minnesota
062016
092016

Cover Photo: Runa Kazakova/Shutterstock Images
Interior Photos: Shutterstock Images, 1, 6, 7, 10, 14, 19; Aleksandra Dabrowa/Shutterstock Images, 5; Nikolai Tsvetkov/Shutterstock Images, 8–9; VP Photo Studio/Shutterstock Images, 11; Kachalkina Veronika/Shutterstock Images, 12–13; Katarzyna Mazurowska/Shutterstock Images, 16–17, 18; Red Line Editorial, 20 (left), 20 (right), 21 (left), 21 (right)

Editor: Brienna Rossiter
Series Designer: Madeline Berger
Art Direction: Dorothy Toth

Publisher's Cataloging-in-Publication Data
Names: Statts, Leo, author.
Title: German shepherds / by Leo Statts.
Description: Minneapolis, MN : Abdo Zoom, [2017] | Series: Dogs | Includes
    bibliographical references and index.
Identifiers: LCCN 2016941147 | ISBN 9781680791730 (lib. bdg.) |
    ISBN 9781680793413 (ebook) | ISBN 9781680794304 (Read-to-me ebook)
Subjects: LCSH: German shepherd dog--Juvenile literature.
Classification: DDC 636.737--dc23
LC record available at http://lccn.loc.gov/2016941147

Table of Contents

German Shepherds

German shepherds are strong dogs. They are one of the smartest dog breeds.

Body

German shepherds have long tails.

Their tails are **bushy**.

Their ears are large.
They stick up.

German shepherds have thick fur. It is usually black and tan.

Care

German shepherds need exercise.

They need a walk every day. They like to be with their human families.

Personality

German shepherds like to learn. They are hard workers. Training them is easy.

They like to have a
job to do.

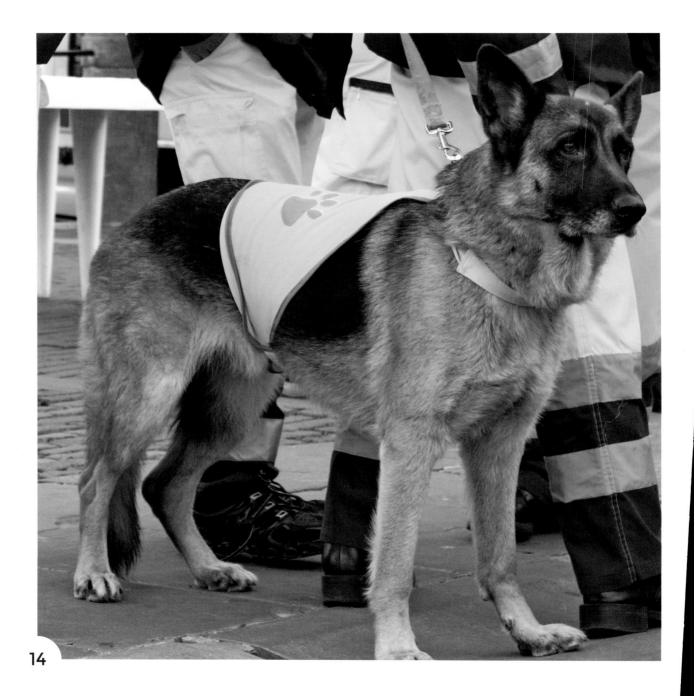

They can be police dogs. They can be military dogs. Some are rescue dogs. Others have roles in TV and films.

The first German shepherds were **bred** in 1889. They were in Germany.

They worked as
farm dogs.

They watched over and **herded** sheep.

Today German shepherds
live around the world.

Average Weight

A German shepherd is heavier than a full suitcase.

85 lbs   50 lbs

Average Height

A German shepherd is more than twice the height of a basketball.

24 in

9.5 in

Glossary

bred - raised so that it will have a special kind of look or feature.

breed - a group of animals sharing the same looks and features.

bushy - full and shaggy.

herded - moved animals together in a group.

training - teaching a dog to do something.

Booklinks

For more information on German shepherds, please visit booklinks.abdopublishing.com

 In on Animals!

Learn even more with the Abdo Zoom Animals database. Check out abdozoom.com for more information.

Index